BUSINESS'S SECRET WEAPON

The Art and Science of List Building

-Ramesh Chauhan

ISBN: 9798302905604
Imprint: Independently published

Dedication

To all the dreamers, doers, and builders of tomorrow's businesses. May this book inspire you to connect, engage, and grow with integrity and purpose.

Epigraph

"The success of a business lies not in its size, but in the relationships it nurtures. An email list is not just a database—it's a community of trust."
— Unknown

Acknowledgments

This book is the culmination of years of learning, teaching, and growth, and it wouldn't have been possible without the support of many incredible individuals.

I am deeply grateful to my students, whose curiosity and ambition have inspired me over the last 30 years. You taught me as much as I taught you.

A heartfelt thank you to my family and friends for their unwavering support during my 15 years as a writer. Your encouragement has been my foundation.

To my readers, thank you for trusting me to guide you through your journey. Your success is my greatest reward.

Finally, to the creators and entrepreneurs who generously shared their experiences and insights for this book, I owe you my sincerest gratitude.

Disclaimer

The information presented in this book represents the views of the author as of the date of publication. While every effort has been made to ensure accuracy, the author assumes no responsibility for any errors or omissions. This book is for informational purposes only and does not constitute professional or legal advice.

Any results or earnings mentioned are examples and not guarantees. Success in email marketing depends on individual effort, experience, and skill. Readers are encouraged to conduct their own research and consult qualified professionals before making decisions based on the content of this book.

Preface

Over the last 30 years as a teacher and 15 years as a writer, I have seen the profound impact of communication on growth—whether in education, personal development, or business. Communication builds bridges, fosters understanding, and drives action.

In the digital age, email has become a cornerstone of communication, yet many fail to harness its potential. This book is my attempt to bridge that gap by providing a comprehensive guide to email list building, a skill that can transform your business if applied correctly.

This is not just a book of theory; it's a toolkit filled with strategies, real-life examples, and actionable insights to help you grow. I hope it serves as a stepping stone to your success.

Prologue

It began with a simple question: "How do I grow my audience?"

In a classroom, a student asked me this, not about business but about making an impact. That question planted the seed for this book. I realized that growing an audience—whether in business, education, or life—requires understanding, trust, and value.

This book is for anyone who wants to create meaningful connections, whether you're building a business or a community. It's about unlocking the power of relationships through the art and science of list building.

The strategies I share here are the same ones I've used and seen others use to achieve incredible results. Let's embark on this journey together and build something extraordinary.

6
BUSINESS'S SECRET WEAPON

CONTENT

Dedication	3
Epigraph	3
Acknowledgments	3
Disclaimer	4
Preface	4
About the Author	5
Introduction: The Hidden Gem of Business Success	11
Chapter 1: Understanding the Power of Email Lists	15
What is List Building and Why It Matters?	15
The Unique Value of Email Marketing Compared to Social Media and Ads	15
The Psychological Edge: Why People Respond to Personalized Emails	16
Chapter 2: The Science Behind List Building	18
The Data-Driven Approach: Metrics That Matter	18
Building Trust: Ethical Practices for Sustainable Growth	19
Common Misconceptions Debunked	20
Part 2: Building Your Business List from Scratch	23
Chapter 3: Preparing Your Strategy	25
Identifying Your Target Audience and Their Needs	25

Creating Value Propositions That Attract the Right Subscribers — 26

Choosing the Right Tools and Platforms for Your Business — 27

Putting It All Together — 28

Chapter 4: Crafting a Magnetic Lead Magnet — 29

What Makes a Great Lead Magnet? — 29

Step-by-Step Guide to Creating Compelling Offers — 30

Case Studies of Successful Lead Magnets — 31

Chapter 5: Designing Irresistible Opt-In Pages — 33

Key Elements of a High-Converting Landing Page — 33

Examples and Templates for Different Industries — 34

Tips for Optimizing User Experience — 35

Part 3: Engaging and Growing Your Audience — 37

Chapter 6: Nurturing Subscriber Relationships — 39

The Importance of Personalization: Addressing Subscribers by Name — 39

Creating Email Sequences That Educate, Entertain, and Convert — 40

Balancing Content vs. Promotion in Your Emails — 41

Bringing It All Together — 42

Chapter 7: Turning Subscribers into Loyal Customers — 43

Using Segmentation to Target Specific Subscriber Groups — 43

Crafting One-Time Offers and Time-Sensitive Promotions — 43

How to Measure Conversion Success	44
Part 4: Advanced Tactics for List Management	47
Chapter 8: Using Double Opt-Ins to Build Trust	49
What Are Double Opt-Ins and How They Improve List Quality	49
Step-by-Step Setup for Double Opt-Ins	49
Avoiding Common Mistakes with Confirmation Emails	50
Chapter 9: Automating for Efficiency and Scale	52
The Role of Autoresponders in List Management	52
Examples of Automated Campaigns for Engagement	52
Tools to Streamline Email Marketing Efforts	54
Chapter 10: Expanding Your Reach with eZines and Newsletters	56
Creating Engaging Content for Recurring Communication	56
How eZines Can Build Anticipation for Products	57
Advantages and Challenges of Running a Newsletter	58
Part 5: Sustaining and Leveraging Your Secret Weapon	61
Chapter 11: Ethical Practices and Compliance	63
Avoiding Spam Traps and Maintaining Credibility	63
Navigating GDPR, CAN-SPAM, and Other Legal Frameworks	64
The Long-Term Value of Building Trust with Subscribers	65

Chapter 12: Maintaining Subscriber Engagement 67

Strategies to Keep Your List Active and Reduce Unsubscribes 67

Leveraging Analytics to Refine Your Approach 68

Re-Engagement Campaigns for Dormant Subscribers 69

Conclusion: Unlocking the True Potential of List Building 71

Recap of the Key Takeaways 71

How to Implement These Strategies Immediately 72

Inspirational Message to Motivate Readers to Action 72

Additional Features for "Business's Secret Weapon: The Art and Science of List Building" 75

Worksheets and Templates 75

Case Studies and Real-Life Examples 76

Actionable Tips in Every Chapter 77

Glossary 77

Final Notes 77

Introduction: The Hidden Gem of Business Success

If you're looking for an invaluable strategy to elevate your business in today's competitive world, you've come to the right place. This guide is designed to give you a head start on mastering one of the most impactful tools in modern marketing—email list building.

If you're new to business or online marketing, you might be asking, "What exactly is email list building?" or "Why is it important?"

The answer is simple: email list building is the process of creating a database of potential customers who are genuinely interested in your product, service, or expertise. These are people who've willingly chosen to engage with your brand, making them far more likely to convert into loyal customers.

Imagine this: You own a website and use a subscription form to collect visitor information like names and email addresses. But here's the challenge—most visitors won't sign up unless they see a compelling reason. That's where the magic of offering value, such as a free resource or an irresistible benefit, comes into play. This creates a win-win situation: your visitors receive something useful, and you gain their contact information for future engagement.

Building a subscriber list is not just a task—it's a foundation for long-term business success. A well-maintained list can open doors to consistent customer interactions, targeted marketing, and, ultimately, a thriving business.

However, like any worthwhile endeavor, list building comes with its share of challenges. You may face resistance or find yourself intimidated by the competition. But remember, success stems from perseverance, strategy, and continuous learning.

In this book, you will learn:

- Why email lists are a "secret weapon" for businesses of all sizes.
- Proven strategies for building, nurturing, and leveraging your list to boost sales.
- Ethical practices to build trust and maintain credibility with your subscribers.
- Tools, techniques, and real-world examples to help you avoid common pitfalls and stay ahead of the curve.

Whether you're starting from scratch or looking to refine your approach, this guide will equip you with the tools you need to succeed. Let's uncover the hidden gem of business success together and build something extraordinary.

Let's begin!

Part 1: The Foundations of List Building

14 BUSINESS'S SECRET WEAPON

Chapter 1: Understanding the Power of Email Lists

Email list building is more than just a marketing strategy—it's the cornerstone of a successful, sustainable business in the digital age. It involves collecting contact information from individuals who have shown genuine interest in your product, service, or content. By building this list, you're not only gathering potential leads but also nurturing a community of engaged customers who trust your brand.

What is List Building and Why It Matters?

List building is the process of creating a database of individuals who voluntarily provide their contact details, typically in exchange for value—whether it's a free guide, exclusive content, or special offers. This group of people becomes your direct line of communication, bypassing algorithms and reaching your audience where they are most attentive—their inboxes.

Why does this matter? Because in a world crowded with marketing messages, email offers a personal touch. Unlike fleeting social media posts or impersonal advertisements, emails allow you to connect directly with your audience, delivering tailored messages that resonate with their interests and needs.

The Unique Value of Email Marketing Compared to Social Media and Ads

While social media and digital ads are powerful tools, they have limitations:

- **Visibility Control**: Social media algorithms often dictate who sees your content. Even with a large following, your reach can be inconsistent. With email, you have complete control. Your messages land directly in the inbox of your subscribers.
- **Cost Efficiency**: While ads require continuous investment to maintain visibility, email marketing has a much higher return on investment (ROI). For every dollar spent, email marketing generates an average ROI of $36, making it one of the most effective marketing channels.
- **Longevity**: Social media trends and platforms can change, and your audience could disappear overnight due to platform policies or shutdowns. Your email list, however, is an asset you own and can rely on regardless of external changes.

The Psychological Edge: Why People Respond to Personalized Emails

One of the key advantages of email marketing is the ability to personalize messages. Personalization goes beyond addressing subscribers by their name—it's about tailoring content to their preferences, behaviors, and needs.

Psychologically, personalized emails create a sense of value and relevance:

1. **Building Trust**: When you show that you understand your audience, they're more likely to trust your recommendations and engage with your content.
2. **Boosting Engagement**: Personalized emails often feel like one-on-one conversations, making recipients

more inclined to open, read, and act on your messages.
3. **Fostering Loyalty**: Consistent, meaningful interactions build long-term relationships. Subscribers feel valued and are more likely to become repeat customers.

For example, instead of sending a generic "Buy Now" email, a personalized message might say: "Hi Ramesh, we noticed you downloaded our guide on marketing strategies. Here's a tailored offer for tools that complement your learning journey."

This kind of attention to detail not only grabs attention but also encourages action, turning casual subscribers into loyal customers.

By understanding the power of email lists, you're not just marketing—you're building relationships, fostering trust, and laying the groundwork for a successful, sustainable business. In the next chapter, we'll dive into the science behind list building, exploring how data and strategies can help you create lists that deliver results.

Chapter 2: The Science Behind List Building

List building may appear to be an art, but beneath the surface lies a strong foundation of science. Understanding the key metrics, applying ethical practices, and dispelling common misconceptions can turn your email marketing efforts into a data-driven powerhouse.

The Data-Driven Approach: Metrics That Matter

In email marketing, data is your guide to understanding what works and what doesn't. To optimize your email list building and campaign strategies, focus on these key metrics:

1. **Open Rates**
    - Definition: The percentage of recipients who open your email.
    - Why it matters: A high open rate indicates that your subject line is compelling and your audience trusts your content.
    - Tip: Use engaging subject lines and personalize them to the recipient. For example, "Ramesh, here's your exclusive guide!"
2. **Click-Through Rates (CTR)**
    - Definition: The percentage of people who clicked on a link within your email.
    - Why it matters: CTR measures how effective your email content and calls-to-action (CTAs) are.
    - Tip: Ensure your CTA is clear, actionable, and relevant to your audience's needs.
3. **Conversion Rates**

- Definition: The percentage of recipients who completed the desired action, such as making a purchase or signing up for a webinar.
- Why it matters: This metric reflects the ultimate success of your email campaigns in achieving business goals.
- Tip: Align your email content with the landing page to create a seamless experience.

4. **Unsubscribe and Bounce Rates**
   - Definition: Unsubscribes represent people leaving your list, while bounces are emails that failed to deliver.
   - Why it matters: High unsubscribe rates could indicate irrelevant content, while bounce rates may suggest outdated or invalid email addresses.
   - Tip: Regularly clean your list and segment your audience to send targeted, valuable content.

Building Trust: Ethical Practices for Sustainable Growth

Trust is the bedrock of any successful email list. Subscribers need to feel confident that their information is safe and that your emails provide value. Here's how to build and maintain trust:

1. **Transparency is Key**
   - Clearly explain why you're collecting subscriber information and how it will be used.
   - Include a visible privacy policy on your signup forms and landing pages.
2. **Deliver Consistent Value**
   - Ensure every email provides something beneficial, whether it's a tip, resource, or offer.

- Avoid excessive promotions that can make your emails feel like spam.
3. **Respect Subscriber Preferences**
    - Allow subscribers to choose how often they want to hear from you.
    - Honor unsubscribe requests promptly to maintain your reputation.
4. **Follow Legal Compliance**
    - Adhere to laws like GDPR, CAN-SPAM, and others that regulate email marketing.
    - Avoid purchasing email lists, as they can damage your credibility and lead to legal consequences.

Common Misconceptions Debunked

1. **Myth: Bigger Lists Are Always Better**
    - Reality: A smaller, engaged list is far more valuable than a large list of unresponsive subscribers. Focus on quality over quantity.
2. **Myth: Automation Feels Impersonal**
    - Reality: When used thoughtfully, automation can enhance personalization and efficiency. For example, birthday emails or tailored recommendations can strengthen relationships.
3. **Myth: Email Marketing Is Obsolete in the Age of Social Media**
    - Reality: Email marketing remains one of the most effective channels, with a higher ROI compared to social media ads. Emails offer a direct and controlled way to reach your audience.
4. **Myth: All Emails Should Sell Something**

- Reality: Not every email needs to push a product or service. Building trust and providing value will create loyal subscribers who are more likely to buy when the time is right.

By focusing on the science of list building, you can ensure your strategies are not only effective but also sustainable. The next chapter will explore how to create a solid strategy, define your target audience, and lay the groundwork for successful list building.

22 BUSINESS'S SECRET WEAPON

Part 2: Building Your Business List from Scratch

Chapter 3: Preparing Your Strategy

Building a successful email list requires more than just collecting email addresses—it demands a well-thought-out strategy. This chapter delves into the critical steps of identifying your ideal audience, creating value propositions that resonate, and selecting the tools and platforms that will power your list-building efforts.

Identifying Your Target Audience and Their Needs

To build a business email list that delivers results, you must first identify who you want on that list. Your target audience comprises the people most likely to benefit from your offerings.

1. **Understand Your Ideal Customer**
    - Ask questions like: Who are they? What challenges do they face? What solutions are they seeking?
    - Use demographics (age, location, occupation) and psychographics (interests, values, pain points) to define your audience.
2. **Research Their Preferences**
    - Where do they spend time online (social media, forums, blogs)?
    - What type of content do they engage with (articles, videos, infographics)?
3. **Craft Your Audience Persona**
    - Combine your research into a clear profile of your ideal subscriber. For instance:
        - **Name**: Priya Sharma

- **Demographics**: 32, small business owner, based in Mumbai
- **Pain Points**: Struggles with finding affordable marketing tools
- **Goals**: Wants to increase sales and brand awareness

By understanding your audience, you can tailor your strategies to attract and retain them effectively.

Creating Value Propositions That Attract the Right Subscribers

A value proposition is what convinces your target audience to join your email list. It's the unique benefit they'll gain in exchange for providing their contact information.

1. **Identify Their Pain Points**
   - What problems are they trying to solve? For example, are they looking for ways to boost productivity or cut costs?
2. **Offer a Solution**
   - Create lead magnets that address these pain points. Examples include:
     - A free eBook: "10 Budget-Friendly Marketing Tools for Small Businesses"
     - A checklist: "Steps to Launch a Successful Online Ad Campaign"
     - A webinar: "How to Double Your Sales with Email Marketing"
3. **Communicate the Benefits Clearly**
   - Show your audience what's in it for them. Use phrases like:

- "Sign up to receive exclusive tips and tricks to grow your business."
- "Download this free guide to start saving time and money today."

4. **Test and Refine**
    - Experiment with different offers and see which resonates most with your audience. Use tools like A/B testing to compare results.

Choosing the Right Tools and Platforms for Your Business

The tools you use to build and manage your email list can significantly impact your efficiency and results. Here's how to select the best options:

1. **Email Marketing Platforms**
    - Look for platforms that offer features like:
        - Automation (welcome emails, follow-ups)
        - Segmentation (grouping subscribers by interests)
        - Analytics (open rates, click-through rates)
    - Popular platforms include Mailchimp, ConvertKit, and ActiveCampaign.
2. **Landing Page Builders**
    - Choose tools that allow you to create professional-looking pages quickly. Examples: Unbounce, Leadpages, or Elementor for WordPress.
3. **Lead Magnet Delivery Systems**

- Ensure your platform can automatically deliver lead magnets like eBooks or guides after someone signs up.
- Tools like Google Drive, Dropbox, or in-platform delivery through email marketing software work well.

4. **Customer Relationship Management (CRM) Tools**
    - If your business involves direct customer interactions, consider a CRM tool like HubSpot or Zoho to integrate email marketing with customer data.
5. **Integration with Existing Platforms**
    - Ensure your tools integrate seamlessly with your website, social media, and other marketing channels.

Putting It All Together

Preparing your strategy is like building the foundation of a house—it determines the strength and sustainability of everything else. By understanding your audience, crafting irresistible value propositions, and selecting the right tools, you set the stage for a list that drives meaningful results.

In the next chapter, we'll explore how to create and promote lead magnets that attract the right subscribers to your list. Let's turn preparation into action!

Chapter 4: Crafting a Magnetic Lead Magnet

A lead magnet is your most powerful tool for attracting the right subscribers to your email list. It's an incentive—a gift that solves a specific problem or fulfills a need in exchange for contact information. When done right, lead magnets not only grow your list but also establish trust and authority with your audience.

What Makes a Great Lead Magnet?

A compelling lead magnet should meet the following criteria:

1. **Specific and Targeted**
   - It should address a particular problem or need of your target audience. Broad or generic offers often fail to attract engagement.
   - Example: Instead of "How to Start a Business," offer "10 Steps to Launch Your First Online Store in 30 Days."
2. **Immediate Value**
   - The subscriber should gain instant benefits. Make it actionable, informative, or entertaining.
   - Example: A checklist for launching a marketing campaign provides quick, practical help.
3. **High Perceived Value**
   - While it's free, it should look and feel valuable. A polished design and thoughtful content go a long way in creating a professional impression.
4. **Easy to Access and Consume**

- Avoid overwhelming your audience. Choose formats that are simple to deliver and quick to digest, such as:
    - **eBooks or Guides**: In-depth insights on a specific topic
    - **Discounts or Coupons**: Monetary value for e-commerce businesses
    - **Exclusive Content**: Videos, webinars, or whitepapers tailored to your niche
    - **Templates and Tools**: Ready-to-use spreadsheets, frameworks, or checklists

Step-by-Step Guide to Creating Compelling Offers

1. **Define the Problem Your Audience Faces**
    - Survey your audience or analyze their behavior to identify their pain points.
    - Example: If your audience struggles with managing time, a "Daily Productivity Planner" could be a great magnet.
2. **Decide on the Best Format**
    - Match your audience's preferences and the nature of the solution:
        - Visual learners? Opt for videos or infographics.
        - Professionals? Provide templates or reports.
3. **Create the Content**
    - Write clear, concise, and actionable content. Focus on solving the problem, not overwhelming it with excessive details.
    - Example: A lead magnet on "Social Media Strategies" might include:

- A 5-step plan to increase followers
- Tools to schedule posts
- Tips for writing engaging captions

4. **Design for Appeal**
   - Use visually appealing layouts with professional fonts, colors, and imagery. Tools like Canva or Adobe Spark can help non-designers.

5. **Deliver Seamlessly**
   - Set up an automated system to deliver the lead magnet immediately upon sign-up.
   - Include a thank-you email to confirm the delivery and express gratitude.

6. **Promote Effectively**
   - Highlight your lead magnet on your website, social media, and through paid ads.
   - Use persuasive copy: "Unlock your free guide to double your productivity today!"

Case Studies of Successful Lead Magnets

1. **Case Study: Digital Marketing Course**
   - **Lead Magnet**: "30 Days of Social Media Content Ideas" (PDF download)
   - **Target Audience**: Small business owners and marketers struggling to create content.
   - **Results**: Over 10,000 downloads in three months, with a 20% conversion rate to paid courses.

2. **Case Study: E-Commerce Store**
   - **Lead Magnet**: 15% off the first purchase (discount code)
   - **Target Audience**: First-time visitors hesitant to buy.

- **Results**: A 35% increase in email subscribers and a significant rise in first-purchase sales.
3. **Case Study: Coaching Business**
    - **Lead Magnet**: Free "Goal Setting Workbook" (interactive PDF)
    - **Target Audience**: Entrepreneurs seeking structure in their planning.
    - **Results**: 5,000 new subscribers in six weeks, with a 10% upsell to a coaching package.

A great lead magnet isn't just about growing your list; it's about attracting the right subscribers who align with your goals. By creating a targeted, valuable, and well-presented lead magnet, you set the stage for meaningful engagement and long-term success.

In the next chapter, we'll discuss how to design high-converting opt-in pages to showcase your lead magnets effectively.

Chapter 5: Designing Irresistible Opt-In Pages

An opt-in page is where the magic of list building begins. It's the gateway that turns visitors into subscribers. A well-designed opt-in page showcases your lead magnet effectively, builds trust, and drives conversions. In this chapter, we'll explore the essential components of a high-converting landing page, provide examples for various industries, and share tips to enhance user experience.

Key Elements of a High-Converting Landing Page

1. **A Clear and Compelling Headline**
    - Grab attention instantly with a headline that highlights the benefit of signing up.
    - Example: *"Unlock the Secrets to Doubling Your Sales with Our Free Guide!"*
2. **Persuasive Subheadline**
    - Complement your headline with a brief, engaging subheadline.
    - Example: *"Get actionable tips and strategies to grow your business in 30 days."*
3. **Visual Appeal**
    - Include high-quality images, illustrations, or videos that represent your offer.
    - Example: A snapshot of an eBook cover or a screenshot of a free tool.
4. **Highlight the Value Proposition**
    - Use bullet points to summarize what subscribers will gain.
    - Example:
        - *Step-by-step actionable strategies*

- Proven tips from industry experts
- Completely free—no strings attached!

5. **A Simple and Visible Opt-In Form**
   - Keep the form fields minimal (name and email are often sufficient).
   - Place it prominently above the fold for easy visibility.

6. **Call-to-Action (CTA) Button**
   - Use an action-oriented CTA that conveys urgency and benefit.
   - Examples:
     - "Download Now"
     - "Get Instant Access"
     - "Start Your Free Trial"

7. **Trust Elements**
   - Build credibility with trust signals like testimonials, security badges, or privacy statements.
   - Example: *"Your email is safe with us—we'll never spam you."*

Examples and Templates for Different Industries

1. **Digital Marketing Agency**
   - **Headline**: *"Supercharge Your Marketing Campaigns with Our Free Checklist!"*
   - **Visual**: A downloadable checklist image.
   - **CTA**: *"Get My Free Checklist"*

2. **E-Commerce Store**
   - **Headline**: *"Enjoy 20% Off Your First Purchase!"*
   - **Visual**: A mockup of the discount voucher.
   - **CTA**: *"Claim My Discount Now"*

3. **Fitness Trainer**
   - **Headline**: *"Transform Your Body in 4 Weeks with Our Free Workout Plan!"*
   - **Visual**: A photo of a person exercising or a sample workout plan.
   - **CTA**: *"Start Your Transformation"*
4. **Coaching Business**
   - **Headline**: *"Achieve Your Goals Faster with Our Free Goal-Setting Workbook!"*
   - **Visual**: A screenshot of the workbook's cover page.
   - **CTA**: *"Get My Free Workbook"*

Tips for Optimizing User Experience

1. **Keep It Simple**
   - Avoid clutter and distractions. Stick to a single, clear message that leads visitors to the opt-in form.
2. **Ensure Mobile Responsiveness**
   - Design your page to look great on all devices, especially smartphones. Over half of web traffic comes from mobile users.
3. **Use Contrasting Colors for CTAs**
   - Make your CTA button stand out with contrasting colors that draw attention.
4. **Speed Matters**
   - Optimize your landing page for fast loading times. Use tools like Google PageSpeed Insights to test and improve performance.
5. **A/B Test Regularly**

- Experiment with different headlines, visuals, and CTAs to determine what resonates best with your audience.
6. **Place Focus Above the Fold**
    - Ensure critical elements (headline, opt-in form, CTA) are visible without scrolling.
7. **Add Exit Intent Pop-Ups**
    - Capture visitors who are about to leave with a pop-up offering additional incentives, like a bonus resource or discount.

By incorporating these elements and strategies, you can create opt-in pages that not only look appealing but also convert visitors into loyal subscribers.

In the next chapter, we'll dive into strategies for maintaining and engaging your audience once they've joined your list. Let's ensure those subscribers become your long-term customers!

Part 3: Engaging and Growing Your Audience

BUSINESS'S SECRET WEAPON

Chapter 6: Nurturing Subscriber Relationships

Growing an email list is just the beginning; the real magic happens in how you engage with your subscribers. Nurturing relationships is about building trust, offering value, and creating meaningful connections that turn casual subscribers into loyal customers. This chapter explores the power of personalization, crafting email sequences that work, and maintaining the right balance between providing value and promoting your offerings.

The Importance of Personalization: Addressing Subscribers by Name

Personalization goes beyond using someone's first name in an email—it's about tailoring content to their preferences, needs, and behaviors. Why is this so effective?

1. **It Builds Trust**
   - People are more likely to engage with a brand that makes them feel understood and valued.
   - Example: *"Hi Ramesh, here's your personalized marketing plan for small businesses."*
2. **It Increases Engagement**
   - Personalized subject lines can boost open rates by 26%. Emails that reference a subscriber's interests or past behavior are more likely to lead to action.
3. **It Enhances Conversion Rates**

- By delivering relevant content, you create a stronger connection, making it easier to guide subscribers toward a purchase.
- Example: Recommending a product similar to one they've shown interest in previously.

Tips for Personalization:

- Use dynamic fields in your email marketing software to include names and other personal details.
- Segment your list based on subscriber behavior, demographics, or preferences.
- Reference their interactions with your brand, like downloads, purchases, or clicks.

Creating Email Sequences That Educate, Entertain, and Convert

An email sequence is a series of automated emails designed to guide subscribers through a journey—from awareness to conversion. Here's how to structure an effective sequence:

1. **Welcome Sequence**
   - Goal: Introduce your brand and set expectations.
   - Emails:
     - Email 1: A warm welcome and delivery of the lead magnet.
     - Email 2: Share your story and the value you provide.
     - Email 3: Highlight testimonials or success stories.
2. **Educational Sequence**

- Goal: Provide valuable insights to position yourself as an expert.
- Emails:
  - Email 1: Share actionable tips related to your niche.
  - Email 2: Offer a free resource (e.g., a blog post or video).
  - Email 3: Answer common questions or address objections.

3. **Engagement Sequence**
   - Goal: Entertain while keeping your audience engaged.
   - Emails:
     - Share a behind-the-scenes look at your business.
     - Include fun facts or interactive content like polls or quizzes.
     - Use storytelling to connect emotionally.

4. **Conversion Sequence**
   - Goal: Motivate subscribers to take action.
   - Emails:
     - Highlight the benefits of your product/service.
     - Include a time-sensitive offer or discount.
     - Add a social proof element (e.g., user reviews or case studies).

Balancing Content vs. Promotion in Your Emails

The key to successful email marketing is maintaining the right balance between providing value and promoting your products or services.

1. **The 80/20 Rule**
    - Spend 80% of your emails delivering value (educational content, tips, stories) and 20% on promotional activities.
2. **Focus on Value-Driven Content**
    - Examples:
        - Tips and tricks related to your industry.
        - Answers to subscriber questions.
        - Free resources like guides, templates, or tools.
3. **Promotions Done Right**
    - Ensure your promotions feel helpful, not pushy. Highlight how the offer solves a problem or adds value to the subscriber's life.
    - Example: *"This week only: Get 20% off our productivity toolkit—designed to save you hours every day."*
4. **Use a Conversational Tone**
    - Write emails as if you're speaking to a friend. This makes even promotional content feel personal and engaging.

Bringing It All Together

Nurturing subscriber relationships requires a thoughtful approach that prioritizes personalization, valuable content, and strategic promotion. By investing in these relationships, you'll cultivate a loyal audience eager to engage with your brand—and, ultimately, support your business.

In the next chapter, we'll dive deeper into strategies for turning these nurtured relationships into loyal customers. Let's explore the power of conversion-focused tactics!

Chapter 7: Turning Subscribers into Loyal Customers

Using Segmentation to Target Specific Subscriber Groups

Effective list segmentation is essential to turn casual subscribers into loyal customers. Segmentation involves categorizing your email list based on specific criteria, such as:

- **Demographics**: Age, gender, location, and occupation.
- **Behavioral data**: Purchase history, website activity, and engagement with past emails.
- **Interests**: Topics or products subscribers have expressed interest in.

By understanding these distinctions, you can craft targeted messages that resonate deeply with each group. For example:

- Offer personalized product recommendations to repeat buyers.
- Send location-specific promotions to increase regional relevance.
- Target inactive subscribers with re-engagement campaigns tailored to their past interests.

Actionable Tip: Use automation tools like Mailchimp or GetResponse to tag and segment your audience dynamically.

Crafting One-Time Offers and Time-Sensitive Promotions

One-time offers (OTOs) and limited-time promotions are powerful psychological triggers that encourage immediate action:

- **Exclusivity**: Highlight the unique nature of the offer. For instance, "Available only to our subscribers for the next 24 hours."
- **Urgency**: Use time constraints to create FOMO (fear of missing out). Examples include flash sales or countdown timers in your emails.

When designing these promotions:

1. Align the offer with subscriber preferences identified through segmentation.
2. Incorporate persuasive language, such as "Last chance!" or "Don't miss this deal!"
3. Ensure a seamless user experience from email to checkout to minimize drop-offs.

Case Study Example: A fitness gear retailer offered a 30% discount on a new product for one day. By targeting fitness enthusiasts who had previously purchased workout accessories, they achieved a 25% conversion rate on the promotion.

How to Measure Conversion Success

To determine the effectiveness of your efforts, monitor these key metrics:

- **Click-Through Rate (CTR)**: Indicates the percentage of recipients engaging with your email. A higher CTR shows interest in your offer.
- **Conversion Rate**: Measures the percentage of email recipients who completed the desired action, such as making a purchase.

- **Revenue Per Email Sent (RPE)**: Tracks the total revenue generated by an email divided by the number of emails sent.

Steps to analyze and improve:

1. Use A/B testing to experiment with subject lines, CTAs, and email formats.
2. Track user journeys from email to purchase using analytics tools like Google Analytics or email platform dashboards.
3. Follow up with non-converters to understand potential barriers, such as unclear messaging or a complicated checkout process.

Quick Win: Regularly refine your segmentation and promotions based on metric insights to maximize conversions and build lasting customer relationships.

By employing segmentation, leveraging compelling promotions, and analyzing conversion success, businesses can transform subscribers into devoted customers, ensuring a sustainable and scalable email marketing strategy.

Part 4: Advanced Tactics for List Management

Chapter 8: Using Double Opt-Ins to Build Trust

What Are Double Opt-Ins and How They Improve List Quality

Double opt-ins are a two-step process where subscribers confirm their interest in joining your email list after initially providing their information. The process involves:

1. **Initial Sign-Up**: A visitor provides their email address and other details through a form.
2. **Confirmation Email**: A verification email is sent to the subscriber, requiring them to confirm their subscription by clicking a link.

Why Double Opt-Ins Matter:

- **Increased Trust**: Demonstrates professionalism and respect for user consent, fostering trust.
- **Better List Quality**: Ensures that only genuinely interested individuals remain on your list, leading to higher engagement and conversion rates.
- **Spam Protection**: Reduces the chances of spam emails, fake sign-ups, or incorrect addresses clogging your list.

Statistical Insight: Lists built with double opt-ins typically have a 30-50% higher engagement rate compared to single opt-in lists.

Step-by-Step Setup for Double Opt-Ins

Implementing a double opt-in process is straightforward with most email marketing platforms. Follow these steps:

1. **Create a Signup Form**:
   - Design an appealing form that captures essential details (e.g., name and email).
   - Include a clear call-to-action (CTA), like "Join Now" or "Subscribe to Stay Updated."
2. **Draft a Confirmation Email**:
   - Subject line: Use an inviting, action-driven phrase like "Confirm Your Subscription to Get Started."
   - Content: Briefly thank the user for signing up and explain the next step. Include a prominent confirmation link or button.
3. **Set Up Automation**:
   - Use tools like Mailchimp, Aweber, or ConvertKit to automate the process.
   - Trigger the confirmation email immediately after sign-up.
4. **Customize the Confirmation Page**:
   - Redirect users who confirm their email to a thank-you page. Offer additional value, such as a free download or exclusive content, as a reward.
5. **Test the Workflow**:
   - Test the entire process by signing up yourself. Ensure that emails are sent promptly, links work correctly, and the experience is seamless.

Quick Tip: Keep the confirmation email and page design consistent with your brand to reinforce recognition and trust.

Avoiding Common Mistakes with Confirmation Emails

To maximize the effectiveness of your double opt-in process, avoid these pitfalls:

1. **Unclear Messaging**:
    - Be specific about the purpose of the email. Use straightforward language like, "Click below to confirm your subscription."
2. **Overloading with Information**:
    - Avoid adding promotions or unnecessary details in the confirmation email. Keep the focus on confirming the subscription.
3. **Poor Timing**:
    - Ensure the confirmation email is sent immediately after the user submits their details. Delays can lead to confusion or loss of interest.
4. **Complicated Confirmation Process**:
    - The confirmation step should be simple—preferably a single click. Avoid asking for additional details at this stage.
5. **Generic Sender Information**:
    - Use a recognizable "from" name and email address. For example, "YourBrand Team" or "."

Best Practice: Include a note reassuring users that their email address is safe and won't be shared or spammed.

By using double opt-ins, you can build a high-quality, engaged email list while establishing trust and credibility with your audience. This process not only enhances the efficiency of your email marketing efforts but also aligns with ethical practices and data protection laws.

Chapter 9: Automating for Efficiency and Scale

The Role of Autoresponders in List Management

Autoresponders are the backbone of efficient email marketing, enabling businesses to maintain consistent communication with subscribers without manual effort. Their key roles include:

1. **Onboarding New Subscribers**:
    - Welcome emails set the tone for the relationship. They provide a warm introduction and share valuable resources or content to engage subscribers from the start.
2. **Building Relationships**:
    - Drip campaigns deliver a series of emails over time to educate, nurture, and establish trust with subscribers, keeping them engaged.
3. **Driving Conversions**:
    - Autoresponders can send timely promotional emails or exclusive offers to encourage purchases.
4. **Maintaining Engagement**:
    - Automated re-engagement campaigns can revive interest among inactive subscribers, keeping your list active and responsive.

Key Insight: Studies show that emails triggered by autoresponders generate 4x more open rates and 5x higher click rates compared to one-time broadcast emails.

Examples of Automated Campaigns for Engagement

To maximize the impact of your email list, consider these types of automated campaigns:

1. **Welcome Sequence**:
   - A multi-email series introducing your brand, sharing your story, and offering a lead magnet or free resource.
   - Example:
     - Email 1: Welcome and thank you for subscribing.
     - Email 2: Overview of your brand or product benefits.
     - Email 3: Link to an exclusive resource or discount.
2. **Educational Series**:
   - A step-by-step guide or tutorial delivered in parts to educate subscribers about a topic.
   - Example: A cooking brand might send "5 Days to Mastering Healthy Recipes."
3. **Promotional Campaigns**:
   - Automate offers during sales events or for product launches.
   - Example: Send a reminder sequence leading up to Black Friday, with escalating urgency.
4. **Re-engagement Campaigns**:
   - Target inactive subscribers with content like, "We miss you!" and offer incentives to return.
   - Example: "It's been a while—here's 15% off to welcome you back!"
5. **Transactional Emails**:
   - Confirmations and follow-ups, such as order receipts or feedback requests, keep customers informed and build trust.

Tools to Streamline Email Marketing Efforts

A variety of tools are available to simplify automation and ensure scalability in your email campaigns. Popular choices include:

1. **Mailchimp**:
   - Features: Easy-to-use templates, autoresponders, and segmentation tools.
   - Best for: Small to medium-sized businesses.
2. **ConvertKit**:
   - Features: Seamless automation for creators with features like tagging and visual workflow builders.
   - Best for: Bloggers, creators, and small businesses.
3. **ActiveCampaign**:
   - Features: Advanced segmentation, CRM integration, and behavioral tracking.
   - Best for: Businesses focused on personalization.
4. **HubSpot**:
   - Features: Comprehensive marketing automation suite, including email and analytics.
   - Best for: Enterprises looking for an all-in-one solution.
5. **Klaviyo**:
   - Features: Specialized in e-commerce with pre-built flows for abandoned carts, post-purchase follow-ups, etc.
   - Best for: E-commerce businesses.

Quick Win: Choose a tool based on your business size, budget, and goals. Many platforms offer free trials to help you test features before committing.

Automation, powered by autoresponders, transforms email marketing into an efficient and scalable strategy. By leveraging targeted campaigns and the right tools, businesses can engage subscribers, nurture relationships, and drive consistent growth—all while saving time and effort.

Chapter 10: Expanding Your Reach with eZines and Newsletters

Creating Engaging Content for Recurring Communication

The key to a successful eZine or newsletter is creating content that consistently engages your audience. Your subscribers should look forward to receiving your emails as valuable and entertaining resources. Here's how to achieve that:

1. **Know Your Audience**:
    - Understand your subscribers' interests, needs, and pain points through segmentation and feedback.
    - Example: If you run a health-focused list, include tips, recipes, or wellness advice.
2. **Diversify Your Content**:
    - Include a mix of informative, educational, and promotional content.
    - Example sections:
        - **Feature Article**: A deep dive into a relevant topic.
        - **Quick Tips**: Short, actionable advice.
        - **Spotlight**: Highlight a product, case study, or customer story.
        - **Call to Action (CTA)**: Drive readers to act, whether to read more, shop, or join an event.
3. **Be Consistent**:
    - Send your newsletter on a regular schedule (e.g., weekly, bi-weekly, monthly).
    - Keep formatting consistent with a recognizable style, tone, and layout.

4. **Interactive Elements**:
    - Add polls, quizzes, or user-submitted content to boost engagement.
    - Example: "Vote for our next product feature" or "Share your story to be featured."

Quick Win: Use templates to create visually appealing newsletters that maintain consistency and professionalism.

How eZines Can Build Anticipation for Products

eZines offer a platform to cultivate excitement and anticipation for your product launches and services. Here's how:

1. **Teasers and Sneak Peeks**:
    - Share behind-the-scenes updates, product development stories, or exclusive previews.
    - Example: "A first look at our new collection dropping next month!"
2. **Customer Spotlights and Reviews**:
    - Build credibility by featuring early adopters or beta testers.
    - Example: "Meet Sarah, who transformed her productivity with our new planner!"
3. **Countdowns and Timelines**:
    - Create urgency by including countdown timers or a timeline leading up to the launch date.
4. **Exclusive Pre-Sale Access**:
    - Reward your loyal subscribers by offering early access to the product.
    - Example: "Subscribers get first dibs—shop 24 hours before everyone else!"

Case Study Example: A tech company used an eZine to drip-feed updates about their upcoming gadget, including design sketches, testimonials from testers, and pre-launch event invites. This strategy resulted in a 35% increase in pre-orders.

Advantages and Challenges of Running a Newsletter

Advantages:

1. **Strengthened Relationships**:
   - Regular communication fosters trust and loyalty among subscribers.
2. **Brand Awareness**:
   - By consistently delivering value, your brand stays top-of-mind.
3. **Cost-Effective Marketing**:
   - Newsletters are a low-cost way to nurture leads compared to paid ads.
4. **Increased Conversions**:
   - Personalized recommendations and CTAs drive traffic and sales.
5. **Content Repurposing**:
   - Newsletters can be repurposed into blog posts, social media content, or downloadable resources.

Challenges:

1. **Time and Effort**:
   - Creating high-quality content consistently can be resource-intensive.
2. **Subscriber Fatigue**:
   - Overloading your audience with frequent emails or irrelevant content can lead to unsubscribes.

3. **Spam Filters**:
    - Poorly designed newsletters or misleading subject lines risk being flagged as spam.
4. **Metrics Tracking**:
    - Measuring success requires attention to open rates, click-through rates, and conversions.

Overcoming Challenges:

- Use automation tools to streamline scheduling and delivery.
- Solicit subscriber feedback regularly to refine content.
- Test subject lines, layouts, and sending times to optimize engagement.

eZines and newsletters are powerful tools for expanding your reach, deepening subscriber relationships, and driving product interest. By delivering compelling content and overcoming operational challenges, businesses can use these platforms to maintain a loyal audience and boost conversions.

Part 5: Sustaining and Leveraging Your Secret Weapon

BUSINESS'S SECRET WEAPON

Chapter 11: Ethical Practices and Compliance

Avoiding Spam Traps and Maintaining Credibility

Spam traps are mechanisms used by email providers to catch unethical email practices. Falling into these traps can damage your sender reputation and even block your emails. Here's how to avoid them and build trust:

1. **What Are Spam Traps?**
    - **Recycled Addresses**: Old email accounts that have been deactivated and repurposed as traps.
    - **Typo or Fake Emails**: Deliberately incorrect emails entered by users to avoid spam.
2. **How to Avoid Spam Traps**:
    - **Use Double Opt-Ins**: Confirm subscribers' emails to ensure validity and intent.
    - **Regularly Clean Your List**: Remove inactive or unresponsive emails to avoid outdated addresses.
    - **Monitor Engagement**: High engagement signals a healthy list. Emails to unengaged users are more likely to trigger spam filters.
    - **Avoid Buying Lists**: Purchased lists often contain spam traps, fake addresses, and uninterested users.
3. **Maintaining Credibility**:
    - Send high-quality, relevant content that aligns with subscribers' interests.
    - Include clear branding and contact information to assure recipients your emails are legitimate.

- Allow easy opt-out options to respect user autonomy.

Quick Tip: Use tools like ZeroBounce or BriteVerify to validate your email list regularly.

Navigating GDPR, CAN-SPAM, and Other Legal Frameworks

Compliance with email marketing laws is not just ethical but also essential to avoid fines and penalties. Here's an overview of key regulations:

1. **GDPR (General Data Protection Regulation)**:
    - **Applies to**: Any organization processing the data of EU citizens.
    - **Key Requirements**:
        - Obtain clear, explicit consent for collecting email addresses.
        - Allow users to access, update, or delete their data.
        - Provide a privacy policy explaining how data is used.
    - **Best Practices**:
        - Use checkboxes for consent (unchecked by default).
        - Clearly outline data usage during the signup process.
2. **CAN-SPAM Act (United States)**:
    - **Applies to**: Commercial emails sent to U.S.-based subscribers.
    - **Key Requirements**:
        - Include a clear subject line and accurate sender information.

- Provide a physical mailing address in the email footer.
- Allow users to opt out easily and honor requests within 10 days.
    - **Best Practices**:
        - Avoid misleading subject lines or clickbait tactics.
        - Include an "Unsubscribe" link in every email.
3. **Other Regional Laws**:
    - **CASL (Canada)**: Requires express consent and prohibits misleading marketing.
    - **PECR (UK)**: Governs privacy and electronic communications, including marketing emails.

Tools for Compliance:

- Platforms like Mailchimp and HubSpot offer built-in features for GDPR and CAN-SPAM compliance.
- Regularly update your terms and privacy policies to reflect legal changes.

The Long-Term Value of Building Trust with Subscribers

Ethical practices and compliance are not just about avoiding penalties—they are fundamental to building trust and sustaining a loyal audience. Here's why trust matters:

1. **Stronger Subscriber Relationships**:
    - When subscribers know their data is handled responsibly, they are more likely to engage and stay subscribed.
2. **Higher Engagement Rates**:

- Trusted senders experience better open and click-through rates, driving campaign success.
3. **Improved Sender Reputation**:
    - ISPs (Internet Service Providers) reward ethical practices with better email deliverability.
4. **Sustainable Growth**:
    - Ethical practices lead to organic list growth and foster brand advocacy.
5. **Adaptability to Future Laws**:
    - A commitment to ethical behavior ensures you are prepared for evolving regulations.

Case Example: A business that clearly communicated its GDPR compliance measures in emails saw a 20% increase in trust scores from customers, leading to higher engagement and retention.

By avoiding spam traps, adhering to legal frameworks, and prioritizing trust-building, businesses can create an ethical email marketing strategy that fosters long-term growth. Compliance isn't just about legalities; it's about earning and keeping the loyalty of your subscribers.

Chapter 12: Maintaining Subscriber Engagement

Strategies to Keep Your List Active and Reduce Unsubscribes

Keeping subscribers engaged is a continuous effort. To maintain an active list and reduce unsubscribes, follow these strategies:

1. **Deliver Consistent Value**:
    - Provide content that solves problems, educates, or entertains.
    - Example: A marketing consultant could share case studies, tips, or industry insights.
2. **Segment Your Audience**:
    - Send tailored content that aligns with the interests and behavior of each subscriber group.
    - Example: Segment by purchase history, engagement levels, or demographic data.
3. **Optimize Frequency**:
    - Avoid overwhelming subscribers with too many emails, but don't let them forget you. Find a balanced sending schedule.
4. **Solicit Feedback**:
    - Periodically ask subscribers what type of content they prefer through surveys or polls.
    - Example: "What topics would you like us to cover in our next newsletter?"
5. **Personalize Content**:

- Use names, past purchases, or browsing history to make emails feel tailored and relevant.
- Example: "Hi Sarah, we think you'll love these new arrivals based on your past picks."

6. **Offer Exit Options**:
   - Allow subscribers to adjust email frequency or topics rather than opting out entirely.
   - Example: A "Manage Preferences" link instead of a straightforward "Unsubscribe."

Leveraging Analytics to Refine Your Approach

Analytics can provide actionable insights to optimize engagement and reduce churn. Focus on these key metrics:

1. **Open Rate**:
   - Indicates the effectiveness of your subject lines and timing.
   - Improve by testing different times, personalization, or urgency in subject lines.
2. **Click-Through Rate (CTR)**:
   - Reflects how engaging your content is. High CTR suggests your CTAs and email design are effective.
   - Experiment with CTA placement, wording, and button colors.
3. **Unsubscribe Rate**:
   - Monitor to identify patterns that lead to disengagement, such as over-emailing or irrelevant content.
4. **Engagement Heatmaps**:

- Tools like Litmus can show which parts of your emails get the most attention, helping refine layouts and CTA placement.
5. **Revenue Metrics**:
   - Measure revenue per email or campaign to evaluate ROI.

Actionable Tip: Use A/B testing to experiment with different email elements, from subject lines to design, to see what resonates most with your audience.

Re-Engagement Campaigns for Dormant Subscribers

Inactive subscribers can be a hidden opportunity. Re-engagement campaigns are designed to bring them back into the fold.

1. **Segment Dormant Subscribers**:
   - Define inactivity based on your business (e.g., no opens or clicks for three months).
2. **Craft Attention-Grabbing Emails**:
   - Use intriguing subject lines like, "We Miss You! Here's 15% Off to Welcome You Back."
   - Content should rekindle interest with updates, offers, or new content.
3. **Incentivize Engagement**:
   - Offer exclusive discounts, freebies, or early access to new products.
4. **Ask for Feedback**:
   - Sometimes inactivity is due to mismatched expectations. Ask, "How can we improve our emails?"
5. **Highlight New Value**:

- Share new features, products, or services that the subscriber might not know about.

6. **Set an End Date**:
    - If a subscriber remains inactive after multiple attempts, consider removing them from your list. This improves deliverability and reduces costs.

Example Campaign:

- **Email 1**: "Is It Goodbye? We'd Hate to See You Go!" Offer a discount or ask for feedback.
- **Email 2**: "Still Interested? Let's Start Fresh!" Highlight new content or features.
- **Email 3**: "Final Call: We're About to Say Goodbye." Inform them they'll be removed unless they engage.

Maintaining subscriber engagement requires a mix of personalization, analytics, and proactive strategies. By continuously delivering value, refining your approach based on data, and running targeted re-engagement campaigns, you can ensure that your list remains active, engaged, and ready to convert.

Conclusion: Unlocking the True Potential of List Building

Recap of the Key Takeaways

Building and managing an email list is both an art and a science, blending strategy, creativity, and ethical practices to achieve business success. Throughout this book, we explored the following:

1. **The Foundations of List Building**:
   - Email lists are invaluable for connecting directly with your audience, offering unparalleled personalization and higher ROI compared to other channels.
2. **Building Your List from Scratch**:
   - A compelling lead magnet, an optimized opt-in page, and a clear understanding of your audience's needs are critical first steps.
3. **Engaging and Growing Your Audience**:
   - Nurturing relationships through personalized, value-driven email sequences builds trust and loyalty.
4. **Advanced Tactics for List Management**:
   - Tools like autoresponders, segmentation, and double opt-ins ensure efficiency, scalability, and list quality.
5. **Sustaining Long-Term Success**:
   - Ethical practices, compliance with legal frameworks, and analytics-driven improvements keep your list active and valuable.

How to Implement These Strategies Immediately

The road to mastering list building begins with actionable steps. Here's how you can get started right away:

1. **Create Your First Opt-In Offer**:
   - Brainstorm a lead magnet that aligns with your audience's needs, such as a free guide, discount, or exclusive content.
2. **Set Up Your Email Tools**:
   - Choose a reliable email marketing platform like Mailchimp, ConvertKit, or ActiveCampaign.
   - Build a simple, high-converting opt-in page.
3. **Plan Your Email Sequences**:
   - Draft a welcome series to onboard new subscribers and a drip campaign to nurture them.
4. **Engage Consistently**:
   - Establish a regular email schedule, providing a mix of valuable insights and occasional promotions.
5. **Monitor and Improve**:
   - Use analytics to refine your approach, from subject lines to content focus, based on subscriber behavior.

Inspirational Message to Motivate Readers to Action

The journey of list building isn't just about growing numbers—it's about creating meaningful relationships with people who trust and value your brand. Your email list is more than a tool; it's your business's secret weapon for connection, loyalty, and growth.

Take that first step today. Every email you send has the power to educate, inspire, and convert. Remember, the most successful entrepreneurs didn't start with a massive list—they started with a commitment to serve their audience authentically.

Your potential is limitless. With the strategies outlined in this book, you have everything you need to unlock the full power of list building. **The future of your business starts with the connections you build today. Go create it.**

Additional Features for "Business's Secret Weapon: The Art and Science of List Building"

Worksheets and Templates

Providing actionable tools helps readers immediately apply the lessons in the book. Here are the key worksheets and templates included:

1. **Opt-In Form Designs**:
   - A collection of sample forms for various industries, including:
     - Retail: "Sign up for 10% off your first order!"
     - SaaS: "Get a free trial when you subscribe!"
     - Coaching: "Download your free productivity guide now!"
   - Include visual examples of forms optimized for desktop and mobile.
2. **Email Sequence Planning Sheets**:
   - A structured worksheet for mapping email sequences:
     - Welcome series: Goals, content themes, and timing.
     - Nurture sequence: Education, engagement, and soft sells.
     - Sales sequence: Urgency-driven emails for promotions or launches.

- Space for notes on segmentation and personalization strategies.
3. **Lead Magnet Brainstorming Checklist**:
    - A checklist to ideate and validate lead magnet ideas:
        - What problem does this solve for my audience?
        - Does it align with my product or service offerings?
        - Can I deliver it immediately in a digital format?
    - Examples for inspiration: eBooks, exclusive webinars, templates, and discounts.

Case Studies and Real-Life Examples

Showcasing real-world success stories makes concepts relatable and actionable. Highlight examples across industries:

1. **Retail**:
    - **Example**: A fashion brand grew their email list by 40% using exclusive early access to sales as a lead magnet.
    - **Lesson**: Offer value aligned with your audience's needs.
2. **SaaS**:
    - **Example**: A productivity app generated 20,000 subscribers by offering a free PDF guide titled, "10 Hacks for Managing Your Day."
    - **Lesson**: Address pain points with practical solutions.
3. **Health & Wellness**:

- **Example**: A fitness coach gained 5,000 leads in two months by hosting a free online challenge and collecting email addresses for registration.
- **Lesson**: Engage your audience through interactive campaigns.

Actionable Tips in Every Chapter

Each chapter includes "Quick Wins," small steps readers can implement immediately to see results. Examples include:

- **Chapter 1**: "Create a list of 10 topics your audience would find valuable. Use these ideas to brainstorm lead magnets."
- **Chapter 4**: "Offer a simple checklist or toolkit as a lead magnet—it's quick to create and highly effective."
- **Chapter 7**: "Run a time-sensitive offer targeting your most engaged subscribers to boost conversions."

Glossary

A glossary provides clarity on technical terms, ensuring all readers, regardless of expertise, can follow along. Key terms include:

- **CTR (Click-Through Rate)**: The percentage of recipients who click a link in your email.
- **Opt-Ins**: A process where users voluntarily provide their contact information to join your list.
- **Autoresponders**: Automated emails sent in response to subscriber actions, like sign-ups or purchases.

- **Segmentation**: Dividing your email list into smaller groups based on specific criteria, such as behavior or demographics.
- **Double Opt-In**: A process where subscribers confirm their intent by verifying their email after signing up.

Final Notes

These additional features not only enhance the reader's understanding but also provide them with practical tools to implement the strategies outlined in the book. By combining actionable insights, relatable examples, and ready-to-use templates, readers will be equipped to build, manage, and scale their email lists effectively.

www.ingramcontent.com/pod-product-compliance
Lightning Source LLC
Chambersburg PA
CBHW071654240526
45469CB00023B/2377